THIS JOURNAL IS MADE WITH LOVE BY DAD

This is my gift to you. It is a keepsake of my life and memories that I hope you will treasure forever.
I Love You Today & Always.
- Dad -

© Copyright
http://www.CaptivatingJournals.com

All rights reserved. No part of this book may be reproduced in any written, electronic, recording, or photocopying form without written permission of the author.

This journal is unique in that it offers dad guided questions, but it also offers dad plenty of space to write his own thoughts & ideas freely.

You will find some blank pages throughout. This is where dad can add photos of his choice, drawings, or use them as space to write even more memories that his child/family will treasure forever.

MY EARLY YEARS

My given names: _____

Date of Birth: _____ @ City/Town: _____

State/Province: _____ Country: _____

Time of day and my weight when I was born:
_____

The reason my parents gave me my name:
_____
_____

Names, DOB of My Parents & Birth City/Country:
_____
_____

My Maternal Grandparents & DOB & Birth City/Country:
_____
_____

My Paternal Grandparents & DOB & Birth City/Country:
_____
_____

* Include dates deceased, when applicable.

MY EARLY YEARS

My first words: _____

Interesting events happening the day/year of my birth:
(local storm, who was President/PM, news stories, etc.)

_____
_____
_____
_____
_____
_____
_____

Below is a picture of me as a young child (or use it as space to write more):

MY EARLY YEARS

Use this space for any photos you have of yourself as a baby, your home, your parents, etc., &/or for more space to write your own ideas.

MY EARLY YEARS

My First Memories as a Young Child:

MY EARLY YEARS

My favorite activities that I did/toys I played with when I was a young child:

INTERESTING $ FACTS

When I was a teen/young adult, this was the cost of various items:

Can of Pop: $

Chocolate Bar: $

Home Purchase &/or Apartment Rental: $

Gallon of Milk: $

Loaf of Bread: $

Tube of toothpaste: $

Movie Ticket Admittance: $

Gallon of Gasoline: $

Insert your own idea here

Insert your own idea here

MY EARLY YEARS

What life was like for me as a child compared to what life is like for children today:

To the world you are a father, but to your family, you are the world.

MY SIBLINGS

I had/have _____ siblings. I was #_____ of all the siblings.

My siblings & their DOB, their spouses (include maiden names): _____

_____

_____

_____

_____

_____

What my siblings and I liked to do as kids:

_____

_____

_____

_____

_____

_____

_____

_____

MY SIBLINGS

More information about my siblings….

MY CHILDHOOD

Use this space for any photos you have of yourself as a child, any accomplishments you achieved, your home, your siblings, parents, etc., &/or for more space to write.

MY CHILDHOOD

How I would describe myself as a child: _____

_____
_____
_____
_____
_____
_____
_____
_____

My favorite books or games:

_____
_____
_____
_____

My favorite music as a kid:

_____
_____
_____
_____

My pets & their names:

_____
_____
_____
_____
_____

MY CHILDHOOD

Use this space for any photos you have of yourself as a baby, your home, your parents, etc., &/or for more space to write.

MY CHILDHOOD

My favorite T.V. shows & movies: _____
_____
_____
_____
_____
_____
_____
_____
_____

Did I have a best friend? If so, who was it?
_____
_____

What did I like to do during summer holidays?
_____
_____
_____
_____
_____
_____
_____

MY CHILDHOOD

Use this space for any photos you have of yourself as a baby, your home, your parents, etc., &/or for more space to write.

MY CHILDHOOD

Places I lived as a child (Towns, Addresses, Dates):
_____
_____
_____
_____
_____
_____
_____

What I most liked or disliked about where I lived:
_____
_____
_____
_____
_____
_____
_____
_____
_____
_____
_____
_____
_____

MY CHILDHOOD

Use this space for any photos you have of yourself as a baby, your home, your parents, etc., &/or for more space to write.

MY SCHOOL DAYS

Where I went to school, how I got to school, grades I attended, my friends, my favorite & least-favorite subjects, what I liked most & liked least about school, etc.

MY SCHOOL DAYS

Use this space for any photos you have of yourself during your school years.

OUR FAMILY HERITAGE

Our ancestry, traditions, & what I want you to know about it:

_____
_____
_____
_____
_____
_____
_____
_____
_____
_____
_____
_____
_____
_____
_____
_____

THE HE♥RT *of a Father* IS THE MASTERPICE OF NATURE

OUR RELATIVES

Use this space for any photos or for more space to write about family history.

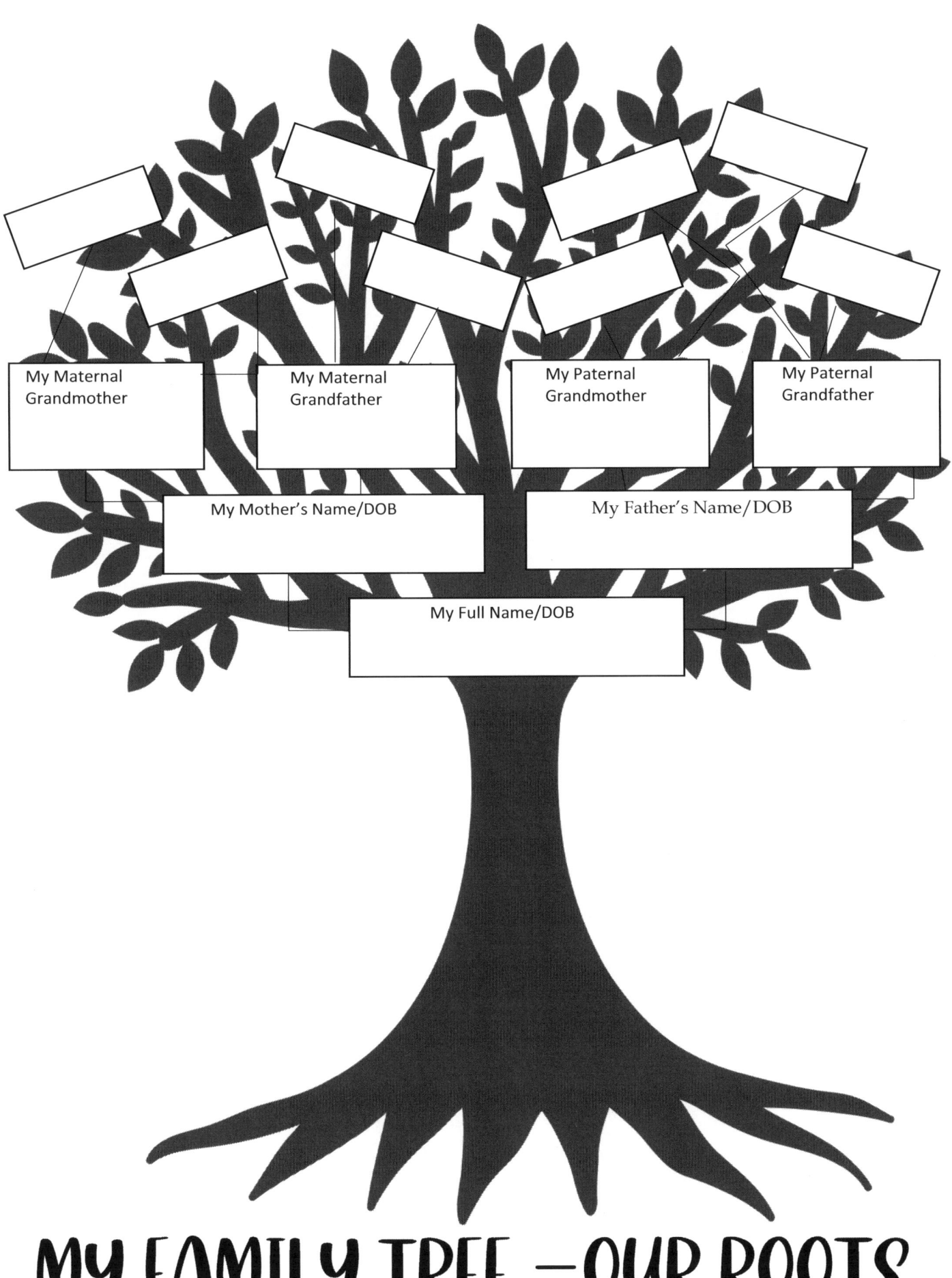

Create your own family tree from scratch if you need to represent divorces or deaths, and resulting remarriages that may have occurred in your family.

My full name/DOB

MY PARENTS (YOUR GRANDPARENTS)

How my parents met:
___

MY PARENTS (YOUR GRANDPARENTS)

How my parents earned a living:
_____
_____
_____
_____
_____
_____
_____
_____

The names of my aunts & uncles (my parents' siblings):
_____
_____
_____
_____
_____
_____
_____

MY PARENTS

Other things I want you to know about my parents that you might not know (i.e. what our family did together, my parents' interests, personalities, their hobbies, skills, hardships they faced,...):

> Fathers hold their children's hands for a short while, but their hearts forever.

PHOTOS

Use this space for any photos of your parents &/or for more space to write.

MY GRANDPARENTS

What I want you to know about my grandparents/your great grandparents:

_____
_____
_____
_____
_____
_____
_____
_____
_____
_____
_____
_____
_____
_____
_____
_____
_____
_____
_____
_____

MORE MEMORIES

Use this space for any photos of your grandparents or others &/or for more space to write.

MY TEEN YEARS

My favorite things, games, hobbies, books, sports, instruments, etc. that I liked and what I disliked when I was a teenager, chores I had, etc.:

My first job & what I had to do:

___

Other jobs I have had & what I have learned from each one:

___

"For all the things my hands have held, the best by far is you."
Unknown author

Use this space for a photo of you as a teen, your family, or for more writing.

MY SPOUSE

How, where, when I met your mother, what I liked about her, etc.:

How & when we got engaged:
_____
_____
_____
_____
_____
_____
_____

Date & time we got married, & what our wedding day was like:
_____
_____
_____
_____
_____
_____
_____
_____
_____
_____
_____

Use this space for a wedding photo or sharing other written memories.

"What can you do to promote world peace? Go home and love your family." – Mother Teresa

OUR LIFE TOGETHER

Our first home, a description of it, its address, how long we lived there, subsequent homes, jobs, choices we made & why, etc.

A father SHOULD BE HIS SON'S ☆ FIRST HERO, ☆ AND HIS DAUGHTERS ♡ FIRST LOVE ♡

"In my life, you are the sun that never fades, and the moon that never wanes."
Unknown author

Use this space for any photos or sharing other written memories.

YOU, MY CHILD

Why we chose your name, my memories of the day you were born, what you liked, didn't like, funny stories, favorite memories, etc..

MY CHILD & OTHER CHILDREN

Memories of my child(ren) growing up & our life as a family…

> "There are only two lasting bequests we can hope to give our children. One is roots. The other is wings."
> — Hodding Carter Jr.

Use this space for any photos or sharing other written memories.

FILL-IN-THE-BLANKS FUN

I love it when my child(ren): _____

I would love to: _____

You are never too old to: _____

I would love to travel to: _____

My favorite song is: _____

My favorite TV show of all time is: _____

My biggest pet peeve is: _____

My favorite saying is: _____

My dream vacation is: _____

My favorite dessert is: _____

My least favorite food is: _____

I got my driver's licence when I was _____ years old

Life is too short. Never put this off until tomorrow:
_____

Insert your own ideas here
_____
_____
_____

ABOUT ME (DAD)

My special skills and talents, what I feel I'm good at, not good at, my favorite family events, my proudest accomplishments, etc.

MORE ABOUT DAD

Some of my favorite memories of my life, & some not-so-favorite memories too:

_____
_____
_____
_____
_____
_____
_____
_____
_____
_____
_____
_____
_____
_____
_____
_____
_____
_____
_____
_____

18 THINGS ABOUT ME...

that you may not know (e.g.) my favorite color, food, season, sport, my coolest adventure, items still on my bucket list, my favorite vacation spots, etc.):

1.
2.
3.
4.
5.
6.
7.
8.
9.
10.
11.
12.
13.
14.
15.
16.
17.
18.

ABOUT DAD

What I learned the hard way in life, and how it has built my character …

Use this space for photos, drawings, or more writing.

"The greatest legacy one can pass on to one's children and grandchildren is not money or other material things accumulated in one's life, but rather a legacy of character and faith." — Billy Graham

ABOUT DAD

The best lessons that I have learned in life that are important for you to know too ….

_____
_____
_____
_____
_____
_____
_____
_____
_____
_____
_____
_____
_____
_____
_____
_____
_____
_____
_____

"Children make your life important." — Erma Bombeck

ABOUT DAD

What I have loved most about being a dad....

"The greatest gifts you can give your children are the roots of responsibility and the wings of independence." — Denis Waitley

The best piece of advice that I ever received:

The best advice I can give you:

"A father is neither an anchor to hold us back nor a sail to take us there, but a guiding light whose love shows us the way." – Unknown

ABOUT ME

What I want you to remember about me always….

ABOUT ME

Things that I know now that I didn't know/understand when I was younger....

ABOUT ME

It is important to live life without regrets and to learn from our mistakes. Do you have any regrets or mistakes you learned from?

MY LETTER TO YOU

What I love about you, what I recognize as your talents, my continued hopes & dreams for you as time passes.

Date: _____

Always my father, forever my hero.

DAD'S WORDS OF ADVICE

Life isn't always easy. Sometimes, it's downright hard. This is how I have overcome adversity in my life, & my tips for getting through the tough times.

DAD'S WORDS OF ADVICE

The most important things in life are….and this is why….and the least important things in life are….

> Life doesn't come with a manual. It comes with a father.

"The best inheritance a parent can give his children is a few minutes of his time each day." — Orlando Aloysius Battista

Find more links of our journals at
https://www.CaptivatingJournals.com